Phyllis ~
Wishing you all the best
in 2013!

Love,
Carroll

Christmas 2012

A Year of *Little Things*

100 SIMPLE WAYS TO BE HAPPY

Caroline Somp

A YEAR OF LITTLE THINGS. Copyright © 2009
by Caroline Somp. Photographs copyright © 2009
by Caroline Somp. All rights reserved.
Printed in China. For information, address
St. Martin's Press, 175 Fifth Avenue,
New York, N.Y. 10010.

www.stmartins.com

ISBN 978-0-312-55762-1

BOOK DESIGN BY DEBORAH KERNER

First Edition: January 2010
10 9 8 7 6 5 4 3 2 1

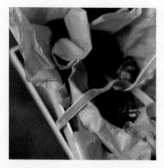

THIS BOOK IS DEDICATED

TO MY GRANDMOTHER,

Anna Carin Holmquist,

WHO WAS MY BEST FRIEND,

ALWAYS SHARING

THE LITTLE THINGS WITH ME.

Contents

Introduction

A year not so long ago, I decided to write down

everything I wanted to have or accomplish

in my life within a certain time period. The

resulting list contained mainly what I call little

things. Everyday experiences that enrich life,

simple pleasures. Small events or thoughtful

moments to mark the turning of the seasons.

Seizing opportunities and choosing to take

responsibility for your life, to be the one behind

the steering wheel.

This book is loosely based on the things in

that list and covers one whole year. It is not

meant to be a book of shoulds. It is meant to

be an invitation to live more deliberately,

to notice what is already unfolding in your life

daily, and to sneak in the spontaneous

and out of the ordinary whenever possible.

Late Winter

1 ⚜ *Dream*

A new year before you like a notebook unopened—crisp, empty pages, straight spine, dreams not dreamt yet, magic unknown. Instead of filling the first page with resolutions, how about something juicy and colorful? Rather than what you should do, what do you want? What dreams flutter in your chest? If you dared, how would life make you feel, where would you be? Aim outrageously high, just to see where you'll end up. Add some empty space for the unexpected, let the possibilities find you. Write a list of what you want in your life. What will this year bring if only you imagine it?

2 ⚜ *Bring Winter Inside*

I want to live deliberately and with awareness, following the seasons and the rhythm outside. Bringing nature indoors is my way of remembering this for every part of the year. Winter in southern Britain is green, but not in a lack-of-snow way, I mean really green. Lushly, deeply, and richly. Graceful ivy dress the trees, brambles weave across the ground, and the moss is a glowing carpet. The curled-up beech leaves covering the forest floor and the few still clinging on the branches balance the greenery with their deep browns. Dainty snowdrops slowly poke their heads aboveground just as winter tightens its grip with frosty mornings and icy winds.

3 ⚘ Sew a Quilt

I dream of whites, browns, blues, and perhaps some green. Soft cotton fabrics, patterns quilted like clouds or leaves, simple edgings and dimensions to spill over the edge a little. Imagine sleeping under something you have worked into being, poured love over, and stitched dreams into. People used to salvage small scraps of fabric from anywhere they could find; the trousers that couldn't possibly be patched one more time, the shirt that had worn too thin, the torn curtains, the children's outgrown clothes, the old tablecloth. Memories of times together were sewn together into something that could be used for a long time still, and be a source of beauty in the home with unique patterns and color combinations. My quilt would be very simple, as I like it, but I'd still sew my life into the pieces.

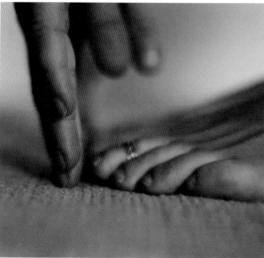

4 ❧ *Stretch*

Do you wiggle your toes in bed in the morning? I do. Rub your eyes? Stretch your arms out? It's a natural thing for the body to want to stretch out. Dogs and cats will have a good, long yawn and a meticulous back stretch before they leave their nap time. Nobody taught them how to do it, their bodies just know. Did you ever ask yours what it might like? No need to follow a book (unless you really want to), just do what feels good. Reach to the tips of your fingers, arch your back like a cat, shake your legs out, hug your knees. Stretch in bed or on the floor, just give it a minute in the morning.

5 ✍ *Create*

Creamy crumbly pastels, neat saturated watercolors, crisp flowing pencil lines. Ballpoint pen doodles in the margin, bright blue, yellow, orange felt-tip, jet-black ink. What would you choose to create with? If you didn't think about it, just let it spread over the page? No need to know how, in fact, even better if you don't. Crimson, violet, sky blue, leaf green—anything goes. Loopy lines, dark blotches, intricate patterns. On the tiniest scrap of paper or with plenty of space. Get your crayons out, play around for an evening.

6 ✍ *Touch Sunlight*

When evening begins in the afternoon and you arrive at work in the dark, every little glimmer of sunshine counts. I walk on the sunny side of the street, turn toward the light at the bus stop, revel in the last rich orange tones of the day, touch the patches of sunlight on the wall. Light and warmth penetrate deep in the winter—let it pat your back, dazzle you softly, tickle the soles of your feet on Sunday mornings.

7 ✽ Write the *Story of Your Life*

If your life was a fairy tale, where would once upon a time begin? Where is the story set—by an ocean? In the hills or a vast city? Is it a beginning full of color and sound or is it quiet and drab? Who are the good guys, what did the villains do? What made the hero or heroine set out on the grand adventure? How did the coincidences add up, where did the winding road go? Who crossed the path, what did they bring? Where is the ending unraveling now? You are the only one who can write this story.

8 · Eat Leafy Greens

I miss green in the winter. Lettuce is replaced by carrots and beets in our salads and the amounts of garden parsley we use tapers down to a sprig for decoration. The leafy greens that stay fresh long into autumn and winter are the exception. They are a conveniently forgotten ingredient in my kitchen with their acquired taste, but every time I give in they surprise me. A blended soup of kale and red lentils is creamy and sweet. One of the best dishes I ever had was spinach koftas fried in chickpea flour. Chard with olive oil, sea salt, and black pepper is delicious in its simplicity. Try them, not just because they are good for you, but because they may surprise you.

9 ✥ *Smell*

Life is rich with smells—faint and subtle or pungent and boisterous. A blooming branch hanging over a fence just begs to be held to your face, fresh bakery bread can stop you midstride, turning toward the salty ocean breeze can bring back more memories than you knew you had. Or perhaps it's the smell of rain on a hot day in July. In winter my sense of smell takes on a different quality. Life is slower and I begin to notice the smells of everyday things— while folding clean laundry, lifting the lid to see if dinner's ready, waiting for snow to fall.

10 ✥ *Winter Flowers*

Come February I begin to long for color, life, and scent. The bright lights and deep colors of Christmas are long forgotten, the simplicity and refreshing bareness of nature will remain a while longer. On quiet, gray days it's my therapy to open the door to a flower shop, pull off my mittens, and breathe in that humid, fragrant air of a space full of plants. Tiny paperwhites, rustling tulips, nodding daffodils. Bright yellow, deep purple, crisp white. Perhaps I'll bring home a pale blue hyacinth bulb to put in a window to bloom. We'll talk about the certainty of spring and rub noses once the fragrance spreads in the room. What are your flower friends in the deep of winter?

11 · *Tea Ceremony*

For me the details are important. It needs to feel right, I need to have a relationship with the things I use daily. I love my flowery teapot and my patterned teacup. They make having a cup of tea into something more. Taking the time to boil fresh water, choosing a mint tea, watching the color seep in and deepen, listening to the pouring, waiting. It's not a conscious ceremony but it follows the same familiar pattern each time, focusing and calming. Do you have a specific routine that is meaningful to you? Preparing your morning coffee, getting ready for bed?

12 ✺ Wear Something Bright

Some days just call for something bright. Something colorful to make the day begin, make it sing. Teal, lemon yellow, soft, mossy green, plum, sky blue, fire-engine red, mauve, rusty orange, turquoise. What delights you? Why not wear it? When you pull on those shoes you beam all day. The scarf that brightens your mood on the way to work. Of course, nobody needs to know that you are bursting in color—those purple socks don't need to show. Only you know what day it is today.

Spring

13 — Celebrate Spring

The Japanese celebrate the blossoming of the cherry trees, *sakura*, as the sign that spring has arrived. Taking precious time off work they go walking among the falling blossoms and spread pale blue picnic blankets beneath the trees. The brief flurry of white and pink is over in a week, a small window of opportunity to marvel at the beauty and brevity of life, always changing. Imagine having a tradition like that every year, in tune with nature's rhythm, a meaningful reminder to live fully. For me, what I wait for in spring are the oceans of bluebells on the forest floor. What would you choose? The first robin singing or perhaps that day when you can finally take your jacket off in the sunshine?

14 — Hop, Skip, Jump

One of my favorite things about spring is when the streets dry up and the sunshine washes down over you, walking along under a deep blue sky. A soft breeze plays with the dust, sweeping, dancing, twirling. It tends to happen at those times, when suddenly it hits you how lucky you are. How beautiful the fresh new green is, how delicious the air is to breathe, how good it is to be alive. The rhythm of your feet surges with your heartbeat and if nobody is looking you are never too old for a skip or a hop. A giddy dance step slipped in, just because.

15 — Sow a Seed

With my lack of confidence I used to think that just because *I* sowed it, a seed wouldn't grow. So I never tried. I know they do now—seeds will sprout, unfurl a transparent root and push one or two round leaves above the surface if I cover them with a little compost and pour water and love. The seed knows what is up and what is down, how to receive light, and how to absorb from the dark. How to grow straight and strong, how to give once it's able. I know too, but don't always remember. I give them homemade paper pots in bright colors (because I'm convinced they grow better that way) and leave them to it.

16 — Sing to Yourself

People used to sing a lot more often, I'm sure. Singing to give rhythm and joy to repetitive work, to get through hard times, to mark seasons and holidays, to give meaning to life's phases, to be together. I used to sing to myself, often letting feelings escape while doing the washing up, walking down a sunny road, while in the shower, mopping the floor, or late at night in bed. The blackbirds in spring inspire me to begin again. Anyone can sing, especially when they're happy, the birds keep telling me.

17  Spring Clean

Once I've swung my windows open to that first mild breeze and the growing light has sought its way into my winter den the dust begins to stand out. I itch to sweep, shake out, air, and throw away. Scrub off the residue of long days indoors, wash clean, and wipe dry. Change the duvets, put away winter clothes, bring out the dry weather shoes. Shoo out the old, let the breeze chase the stale air through the house, give away things you no longer want. See the world through sparkly clear windows and go to sleep in clean sheets.

18 *Plan a Surprise*

Can you keep a secret? *Shh*—don't tell anyone. Not just yet. Let it grow, keep it hidden, snug in the dark. It will gather power and mystery, carried around with you. Stretch its roots a little deeper, unfurl a leaf or two. Is it something colorful? Vibrant or subtle? Will it make her laugh? Will he know exactly what it means? Will it change your life, the audacity of it? Let it be, however small the surprise, don't let it out so soon.

19 *Sew an Apron*

I love pockets. Pockets mean safe, secret little places that are seemingly simple and orderly compartments but when you peek over the edge reveal hidden worlds. Belongings that make up your home away from home like that notebook or favorite lipstick or a forgotten handful of acorns. In spring I'd like to sew an apron for spring-cleaning or gathering herbs in the garden or just puttering around. It would need to have a deep and wide front pocket to plunge my hands into.

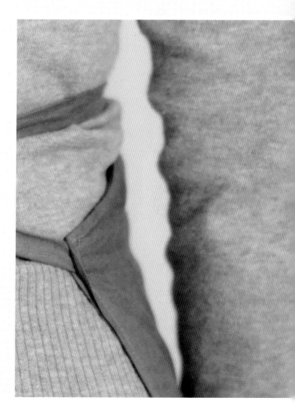

20 ⁓ Be Inspired

Spring is like another beginning of the year. What has been growing, building up, and maturing in darkness and silence during winter is about to be expressed. Life is shifting, decisions are made, and beginnings begun. Where do you want to go? What dreams are still sitting on the shelf? Open up your imagination, be inspired to do more than you thought possible. Look for things that resonate. Images of what you dream of but can't express, photos that make your skin tingle, magazine cutouts that speak to you. Put them where you can see them—on the wall, inside a cupboard door, hung up above your desk, on your bedside table.

21 ⁓ Bring Spring Inside

That first tender green, the tiny and the barely noticeable, small specks of color. Tiny leaves unfolding, soft, the size of mouse ears. I brought a twig of hawthorn inside with me. The little white flowers close to the dark barren stem remind me of Japanese paintings with plum blossom branches. A shy beginning to the season of restless growth. What would you pick? The first crocus, a birch branch?

22 🙠 *Pause*

Birds singing their hearts out, buds bursting, the
sunshine staying up late, and ideas growing in your
head—spring with all its restless let's-go will bloom
around you in a flurry. Why not pause and smile at
it all for a while? Smell the earth waking up, listen
to the breeze in the new leaves, watch the twigs
carried off to nests, feel the tender warmth of a
cloudless sky. Stop on your way to the car, sit down
on that park bench, lean on the porch rail. Breathe
in and move on.

23 ✤ *See*

Once you begin paying attention, they're hard to ignore. The details, little things. Spring is full of those—there by the roadside or in the treetops if you want to notice them. We see all day, sight is our most used sense, but it is easy to see the same things we see every day. Children are experts at seeing the overlooked, and anything can be intriguing if you come close enough. Or look with different eyes, as if you've never seen it before. Your way home from work, have you really seen it? If you turn your head to the right where you normally look left, what would you see? What flutters from the third-floor window? What grows in the cracks of the sidewalk?

24 ✤ *Tender New*

A perky green salad with arugula and cress, tiny radishes, new potatoes with butter. From your own plot or from the farmer's market, those first tender vegetables of the season deserve a meal all to themselves. It used to truly be the first green after a long winter when local produce was all that was available. People longed for lettuce leaves, succulent tomatoes, cucumber, and tender beans in their pods. What couldn't be pickled or stored in cool cellars was absent. Cherish the freshness, winter is over.

25   *Cleanse*

Once spring breaks loose and the ground thaws, I blink in the bright light and feel like shaking off that winter feeling. A little bit sleepy, sluggish, and slow. I want to get moving, flush out the toxins, cleanse and build up afresh. Make sure I get enough vitamins and minerals, colorful fruits and vegetables, tall glasses of clear water. Scrub my pale winter skin, turn my nose to the shy April sun. Nudge my legs out for walks, draw long, deep breaths. Feel new.

26   *Write Letters*

By the time you pull a letter out of its envelope it has gathered so much anticipation and significance. Someone spent time thinking about you over that sheet of paper, wrote down what was meaningful to them, folded, sealed, and addressed it to you. Stamps were stuck on, perhaps they were intricate, perhaps they were plain. And then, once let go into a mailbox, the places that letter went that neither of you know about. The distance it covered with a content that was held in many hands but never read until now. Send more colorful envelopes out into the world.

27 *Find Your Spot*

Find a place to claim as yours. A place to go when you need to be on your own, to get inspiration, think something through, or just be. A place where the most original ideas spark to life, where you feel rejuvenated and clear. It may be an old oak only you know, a bench in a busy park, the perfect overview of the city, a café where you blend in with the crowd, the very end of the pier. As long as you feel it, when you turn the corner and it greets you with that soothing feeling, like coming home. You can carry it with you any-where after a while, like a portable safe space, there when you close your eyes.

28 *Organize*

Boxes and bags, drawers, jars, bowls, and pockets—anything that can hold and carry has a certain magic and power to it. Perhaps it's the order and simplicity that comes with things being tucked away and everything having its own place, combined with the satisfied feel-ing of lifting a lid to reveal treasures. All sorts of colors in that satchel with my art supplies, a heavy, reassuring sense of quality about the camera equipment box, the tinkling of buttons and beads in the mason jar. I believe the space opened up by organizing and putting away invites delightful things you never knew life had up its sleeve. Find a collection of pretty boxes (some old, some new) and organize away to invite something new.

29 ⚬ Do It Differently

In spring you can afford to shake things up. The days are longer and life feels lighter. In the darker months habits are hard to break, they serve to comfort and carry us through, but now you've made it here and a long summer is ahead of you. What are you ready to do differently? A gentle walk in the sunshine wouldn't feel like exercise, today could be the first day. Order an organic vegetable box from a local farm or co-op, have one less cup of coffee. Check off every small step and enjoy the ride.

30 ⚬ Create a Vegetable Garden

Sometimes it helps to focus on the very concrete and simple, literally down to earth. Creating a vegetable garden can be a grounding and therapeutic way to spend some time each day with one's hands in the soil. Sowing radish seeds, planting onions, weeding beds, harvesting string beans, watering the lettuce. Being in touch with the seasons changing, seeing the small labors you make gradually add up, like little steps in the right direction, can be rewarding. Bringing something, however small, to fruition can be very healing and satisfying.

31 *Remind*

I can be rather clumsy, living life faster than my limbs can coordinate, and I let myself know it frequently. Do you have one of those harsh voices in your head pointing things out too? Most of us do. I find it's worth writing little notes to her, reminders. About the things that don't get said—all that you already are, dreams of what you will be. Do you have dainty feet, grow the best tomatoes, sing out of tune in the sweetest way? It's like affirmations, but your very own. Include gratitude for what you have and outrageous wishes that will inspire you on a day when you need it. Write it down, color it in, and keep it in a neat box somewhere nearby to read and remind yourself.

32 *Celebrate an Ordinary Day*

Do you have those dull empty days in March too, when there is nothing much to look forward to and nothing much happening? Spring is feverishly at work in the roots and the sap, but outwardly the world seems to never change, caught in a gray in-between. No snow, no green. Life isn't boring, just unremarkable. Those days call for something special, even if it is just to celebrate the ordinariness. Bake a birthday cake, pop real popcorn for a matinee showing, or have a pillow fight. Because it's the second Thursday of the month.

33 — Go to the Woods

There is a green you see only
once per year. If you go to
the woods or the park under
the translucent and tender
new leaves you already know.
The light sifting through the
forming canopy flickers and
dazzles and there is a muffled
acoustic, whispers, and rustles.
Shoots are unfolding, small
plants spread a blanket over
the ground. The air is fresh
with humidity and endless
possibility, ideas taking shape
to the rhythm of your feet.
Birdsong trilling high above, an
opening ahead, deer bounding
away. Go to the woods before
the season changes.

34 ❧ Keep in Touch

Every time I send a letter to my grandfather it makes his day, but it only happens a few times per year. Time flies and the ones that mean the most sometimes get less time with us than our work colleagues. I want to speak to my brothers, call my parents, get to know my cousins better. Reply to that letter a friend sent me long ago, reconnect with the people who made a difference to my life. Who would make your life richer if you got back in touch? Who deserves a handwritten hello? It doesn't take much.

35 ❧ Wag Your Tail

Dogs tend to live life to the fullest—racing off with ears flapping or immersing themselves in an irresistible smell. Straightforward and down-to-earth, scratching what itches, eating when hungry, and watching everything with curiosity, head tilted just so. They can walk up to strangers for an affectionate scratch or greet new friends in the park with an exuberant play pose—"Why, hello!" I like friends like that. They remind me to wag my tail. Who do you play with? Cats that light up when you enter the room, canaries that chirp in your ear, the horses on the other side of the fence, a playful rabbit? It's all good. Spend some time together and remember what simple living is like.

36 ✦ Give a Hand

With energy increasing in spring it's a good time to volunteer. Visit a retirement home and hold a hand that doesn't get held very often. Light up someone's lonely day, however short the time spent is. Offer to teach someone how to paint, sew their own clothes, or bake the best pie. It may give you back more than you ever put into it.

37 · Fill a Notebook

When I was sixteen a quote stuck with me and I had it written in ballpoint pen on the back cover of my calendar for years. "Don't push the river" it said. Let life take its time and flow with its own rhythm, I guess it means. Though the meaning kept changing for me and I still can't say I know what it means. I looked at those words often and somehow the other quotes and poetry that entered my life also wanted access to that calendar, seeping into the note pages at the back, spreading over the addresses and finally into the dates. And rightly so, I think—poetry and wise words should be at the heart of life. I'm giving them a book of their own, having thrown away that beloved calendar years ago. Give them a space, the words that inspire you.

Summer

38 · Cycle

The places you can go in the summer when you have a bicycle. A vintage cruiser with a laidback seat and tall handlebars. A wicker basket for the Saturday market produce, a spacious carrier for the library books. A blue bike with high wheels and a creaky saddle, swimming trunks, and a packed lunch in a pannier. Roll downhill on city streets, along gravel roads, seafront esplanades, through woods and golden rapeseed fields. Watch the trees and buildings swish by, lean into the turns, give a last push to that uphill slope.

39 · Go on a Picnic

You spread that blanket and suddenly there is a space for something to happen, a home under the trees. Plates and tubs and glasses appear from a wicker basket and so many little dishes. Filled sandwiches, olives, potato salad, slivers of melon, cherries. I still find eating with my fingers and picking this and that childishly satisfying. Lick your fingers and lie back with your feet on the grass. Look up to the summer clouds and listen to the breeze in the leaves.

40 ᴄᴏᴏ *Start a Collection*

The best collections are the living kind, the ones that fluctuate in numbers. You find a perfect piece to add to it but that same day you give another away to someone for whom it was meant to be. Cards are my favorite thing to collect, little pieces of art. They come and they go as I send or give them away. Some stay with me for years, some only pass through. Smooth beach stones tend to find my pocket in the summertime, and I am also partial to houseplants that look like little trees, rubber balls, and thin, satin ribbons. What do you collect?

41 ❧ Walk Barefoot

I read once of a Native American woman who was encouraged to wear shoes, and her explanation as to why she would never pull them on again— "My feet become blind." I wonder what my feet would see if I let them? Hard, sun-warmed pavement, the whisper of rough grass sweeping past, the tickle of short-shorn lawn. The cool of soft plants in the shade, slippery puddle water trickling up between the toes, the insistent pressure of pebbles, the rugged bark when climbing a tree.

42 · Stay Up All Night

Sometimes you stay up so late that it makes no sense to go to bed. Perhaps you are making your way home in the blushing dawn after a night out, or have finally fallen quiet after a night of talking. A riveting story keeps you turning pages until the early hours and come the last sentence you are too touched to fall asleep. Nighttime is a rare time, an opportunity to be truly alone, but not. Someone snoring softly beside you or stirring in the other room. Your neighbors sighing in their sleep. The city is asleep but for a light here and there. Stay awake, let the dark soothe your eyes and your mind. Feel the rhythm of a whole day and night.

43 · Peaches and Cherries

A paper bag of bloodred cherries used to last us kids a long time, sitting on the porch spitting out cherry pits. It was a luxury that happened only then and you knew that it was the summer holidays for sure. There would be cool, yellow nectarines, firm ones, and fuzzy peaches too. The first strawberries of the year and the last at the end of the season. Blueberries and stained fingers, gleaming red currants, soft raspberries, and gooseberries. Tart plums later on and blackberries by the time school started up again. What fruits make it summer for you?

44 *Utterly Ridiculous*

Cloudless, lazy days, garish colors, and melting ice cream—summertime teases you to let up. Leave your serious side indoors for a day and set out to do something utterly ridiculous. Make a fool of yourself on the beach, run screaming around the house, pull your goofiest face. Let people watch, we don't care today. Wear that hat, play that outlandish music, and dance any which way you like. Giggle out nonsense, tickle him to hiccups, and go bonkers. Sometimes it's just the sane thing to do.

45 *Gather*

When I pass by elderberry bushes on summer walks, I'll tiptoe, bend a branch, and pluck a white flower bunch or two. They'll snow pale yellow dust on your hand and give off fruity aromas. I steep them in hot water and sip as is, fresh herbal tea. It reminds me of an old-fashioned cordial, and I think of all the wild plants and flowers people used to know and gather. Elderberry is good for colds, tender nettles make a nourishing soup, rose-hips are good supplements of vitamin C in the wintertime. What do you know of and gather?

46 (page) Love the Rain

Did a summer rain ever drench your hair? Rivulets running down your face, eyelashes wet and sparkly. Your clothes would be soaked by now, but summer showers are warm and fleeting. Look up and let the clouds touch your cheeks, cool fingertips brushing your forehead. Open your hands and let it pour. The patter of drops intensifies until it pounds the ground, happily creating puddles and streams. But July skies have a sense of humor, before you know it cracking open in a bright smile.

47 (page) Bring Summer Inside

I bring in peonies with their heavy silky heads, petals that whisper if you lean in close. Antique roses with delicate scents, peach, white, and pale pink. June and July with their balmy shimmering days, warm bare feet, the hem of your dress catching on a thorn. I bring flowers in all summer—pale yellow cowslip, happy orange calendulas, forget-me-nots, mauve poppies. Fill up small jugs, jam jars, water glasses. Textures like velvet, creased paper, satin. What are the colors of summer where you live?

48   Go Thrifting

I look for teacups with scalloped edges, wood-handled tools, and corduroy skirts. What do you look for? Vintage children's books, silver spoons, or balls of heather-colored yarn? Finding something that was loved and given away is for me more satisfying than buying it new. Vintage things have quality and character and grow worn with grace. Lose yourself in thrift shops or flea markets where everything is unique, one of a kind—you never know what treasure is waiting to be discovered. What will you find today?

49   Have a Garden Party

Hang jam jar lanterns in the trees, spread white cloth over a table in the garden. Pick flowers, lay out the plates. Let the evening sky deepen and the breeze die down while you prepare the main meal. Put on that paisley dress and stick a daisy behind your ear. The guests are due any minute and the lanterns need to be lit. The stars will come out later on, when the dessert is nearly finished. The soft balmy night air is still and the last blackbird to go to sleep joins in the conversation.

50 ✍ *Write Lists*

Lists can get you through anything. Offering clarity for overwhelming information, a structure of to-dos in priority order, encouragement on days
when getting out of bed deserves a check mark. In the summer it might be
all the exciting things not to be missed or forgotten. Lists have power and
potential—for dreams on their way to reality, day-to-day tasks that need
acknowledgment, or just for the love of listing what is meaningful for us. A
row of beautiful things, an outrageous wish list (imagination costs nothing),
insights collected so far, what to pack for that much-longed-for time away.
Then cross out and let go.

51 ✍ *Celebrate Your Body*

What's great about your body? What makes you think, "Hey, that's not bad!" The way
your hair curls on good days, the strength in your legs, how quick your fingers are to
type? Do you have a graceful way of moving your hands, the sweetest frown when you
concentrate, a straight back? Celebrate something about your body, however insignifi-
cant it seems to you. Sink into the feeling of having something worthwhile, hold yourself
with confidence, if only for a minute.

52 · Celebrate Summer

The first butterfly to flutter past makes it summer for me. Lemon yellow wings, a whisper of sultry days ahead. Bright orange, peacock blue. They have flown out of hiding to unfold their wings in the growing sunshine and soon I too can feel the warmth. Sky blue, lacy white edges. I'll wear my summer dresses and sandals, walk down the lane with them winging ahead. I'll pause on the hill with the best view, listen to the skylarks, and count the fields I can see—swaying barley, glowing rapeseed. The breeze tugs at my sleeve and I smile back. It's summer and this is my celebration of it, the first walk of the season.

53 ❧ Wind Down

Traditionally in Sweden people in the countryside used to have a routine of something commonly called "kura skymning," meaning "crouching dusk." It would literally be crouching at dusk—squatting wherever they were outside or curling up by the window indoors. Watching dusk descend, the light fade, and night roll in with the cool, humid breeze. Staring at nothing, listening to the sounds of nature quieting down, wrapping up the day. It must have been a natural way to wind down, an allowance to cease work as the sun turned off the lights and slowed the pace, a transition period to reflect on what is being left behind. With electric lights it is tempting to keep up the momentum of the daylight hours and carry on, but perhaps tonight I will be gazing out the window.

54 *Swim*

Summer means being in the water for me. I grew up by the sea so you'd find me on the smooth rocks leading down to the water, letting the dappled surface dazzle, listening to the waves cluck contentedly. Feeling the sunshine warm my shoulders, the cool waters rising with each step. Up to my waist with swells softly circling and rolling past. Take a deep breath and slice the surface—bubbles and green glassy depths, suspended in silence and heartbeat. Pop your head out and splash around. Where do you swim? In a tranquil lake, crashing Atlantic tide, the deep end of the pool?

55 *Herbs*

Lavender, sage, rosemary, thyme. I'll pinch a twig or leaf on my way past, rubbing the scent into my fingertips, breathing in. Lemon balm soothes anxiety, as does lavender. Rosemary and mint wakes you up and cleanses. Sage and thyme have antiseptic properties. Growing herbs in small terracotta pots on the windowsill can be enough for a tiny medicinal garden. Reach for a leaf of mint for indigestion, a sprig of lavender when stressed. Read up carefully on the use of each and add a few just for the fragrance.

56 · Eat Outside

Open the patio doors, plop down on the front steps, spread a blanket in the garden, set the table under the apple tree. Bring plates and forks and have lunch outside. Pretty much anything tastes better in the open air. You can wiggle your toes in the grass, watch the swallows swoop, let sunlight dapple over the grapes and the butter and crusty bread. When the shade moves closer, it's time to clear the table but not wash up. Stay outside a little longer, the conversation has only just begun.

57 · Wake Up Early

Next time the June sunshine wakes you up early, look out the window. The day has already begun out there—birds warbling in the hedge, a cloudless sky, the smell of lilacs on the wind. Nobody else is awake, tiptoe down the stairs and gently close the door behind you. The stillness is all yours, long before anyone will stir. Enough time for a barefoot walk in the dew and a cup of tea on the back steps.

58 ✤ Enchanted Gardens

Closed-off gardens are so intriguing—doesn't it make you want to peek through the hedge, tiptoe by the fence? An overgrown corner, a mossy branch, pale pink roses climbing the back wall. A canopy of lilacs, a wooden chair, silvery with age. Bells tinkling somewhere, water pouring, I wonder where this path leads? Orchards of gnarly pear trees, a swing. An old white-gabled greenhouse, orange trees in pots, seedlings all lined up. What gardens are there to get lost in close to you?

59 ☙ Do Something Up

When I have a project, I can be absorbed for hours—sanding down the wood until it's silky soft, applying careful strokes of blue paint, pulling the last stitch of woolen yarn on a mended pullover, fitting reclaimed driftwood together for a cabinet. You make it yours—something you found discarded, collected on the beach, bought for nothing, dug out of your closet. You make it beautiful the way you want it and use it, see it everyday. Mend, do up, and create. What is your next project?

60 ☙ Stargaze

Mild summer nights were made for sitting on the front steps or wrapped up in bed by the open window under the starry skies. The black is so soft when the air is warm, reaching down and enveloping you. Surging upward into millions and millions of bright points, a world of dark velvet and sparkle. Bring quilts and pillows to the garden and sleep outside. Fall asleep under the endless ceiling.

61 · Sense of Touch

A mild breeze teasing your hair, gasps of cold water at the beach, loose clothes skimming your skin, crisp dripping watermelon slices—what does summer feel like to you? Any time of year, sensation is literally at your fingertips. What does it feel like to be alive, to touch, to feel? To slip socks on in the morning, hold your breakfast bowl, be jostled gently on the train? Put your hand on someone's shoulder, push a door open. Weigh a glossy orange in your hand, ease into clean, cool sheets, feel alive.

62 ❦ Follow Your Intuition

What would happen if you followed that impulse and spoke to the stranger in the supermarket line? Or followed the less sensible route that you decided against? It can be a wonderful thing getting lost—how will you find what you never looked for otherwise? Spontaneously turn down the most alluring side street, choose the redder dress, follow your intuition for a day. Tell someone how you feel, risk it. Go ahead even though you have no idea how your dream will work out, trust that gut feeling. You'll know.

Autumn

63 *Reinvent Yourself*

The changes in autumn that blow in with the fresh westerly wind, opening up clear high skies and crisp mornings full of promise, make me want to reinvent myself. The leaves dance off the branches in their boldest colors and I want to have a twirl too, learn to dance, wear deep reds and purples, go somewhere I've never been before. Cut my hair, sing out loud, write poems. Begin something new, go after that dream, start off in a different direction. What will you dare this autumn?

64 *Knit*

Soft merino wool, wispy mohair, rustic tweed. Tugging at a ball of yarn, gradually transforming a length of string into something to wear amazes me each time. Knitting is a loved pastime for me, something I pick up again in the fall, whereas for my mom and grandmother having a sock on the needles was a skill that was part of life. These days you can find almost any wool you'd like and knit something just for fun. It's not that difficult, try it. Choose the texture and shade of yarn you want, tuck your legs under in the armchair, and cast on a scarf. It will grow quickly with a plump yarn and there are no instructions to follow, just decide the width.

65 · Clear Out

Just like spring has a thorough tidying, autumn is a good time for clearing out. Letting go of belongings that no longer serve you, recycling what can be reused, throwing away what is too far gone. Be daring in your sorting, placing things in the give-away pile before thinking too hard on it. You'll feel so much lighter afterwards. Creating space in your home opens up possibilities for something new to happen. And you might make somebody happy with that cardigan you never wore.

66 · Wrap Up Warm and Walk

Fresh, windy days chasing plump clouds across the sky just cry out for a long walk. You wrap up warm, pull on a woolen jacket and boots, set out in whatever direction looks most enticing. Perhaps you decide to walk to the crossing, but when you get there the bend to the right is calling you so you go a little farther. Once you're on that forest path, it feels like you could walk forever and you enter a field and then another one, in a wide loop eventually heading home, breathing deeply under the expanse of an open sky.

67 Forage

An apple that has rolled into the street, chestnuts fallen along a forest path, plums hanging over a fence, mushrooms from your secret spot, or the pears your neighbor has too many of each year. Do you go foraging in the autumn? Filling apron pockets with heavy fruit, watching the level of perfect gleaming berries rise in a bucket, making a pie with rhubarb that you picked moments before. These days it's a luxury to receive our nourishment directly from the earth and not through a supermarket. Make the most of it—what grows around the corner from you?

68 Daydream

Daydreaming has an undeservedly bad reputation. What would seem to be doing nothing is in fact one of the most productive things you can do. Letting your mind rest from applied thinking and allowing imagination to take you away can restore clarity and spark ideas. Rather than turn the television on, why not close your eyes and fly off to a Moroccan bazaar, an ancient forest, a friend on the other side of the world. Imagine being a dragonfly or living as a gypsy. Wander freely and return with a fresh mind.

69 Those Before You

What do you know about the people who came before you? What connection do you have with your grandparents, with their parents before them? I have a photo of my grandmother as a five-year-old, riding a tall, stocky workhorse, smiling out of the black-and-white. She lived on a farm during World War II. My great-grandmother made lace-trimmed pillowcases by hand and though I never got to know her, they are spread out in my apartment. My father's parents fled from Estonia during the war, and I have stories of crossing the Baltic Sea at night, ornate hand-knitted mittens, and a love for dense sourdough bread. Does something of your great-grandparents live on in you?

70 · Get to Know a Tree

Autumn is an excellent time to get to know a tree. Trees are only too happy when people come to see them. They spread their branches lovingly over your head and let you lean on their trunk. Go looking for one that for whatever reason speaks to you, where you could imagine sitting for a while. Bring a book, a drawing pad, or your knitting if you want to. Trees don't need to fill conversation, they're content just being there. They'll let sunshine filter down, rustle their leaves in the breeze, and hum a slow song with you.

71 ✢ Go on a Journey

I think I love traveling the most. Even more than arriving. To curl up next to a window on a train or bus and watch the world pass by while falling into a quiet contentment. It's time spent doing something (traveling), so it's a rare opportunity for doing nothing without feeling bad about it. Perhaps it's the gentle rocking and the ever-changing landscape, the muffled sounds and soft secluded seat; a view to everything from a place of complete safety that makes me feel calm and perfectly content. Like a child being carried, sinking into the movements of the parent, required to do nothing but watch and enjoy.

72 ✢ Bake

Open your window and let the promise of apple pie swirl down the street. Dull, overcast days can completely turn around by pulling something you baked out of the oven. Let the smell spread its magic through the house. Blueberry crumble, soft cinnamon rolls, a whole grain crusty loaf. Lemon tart, walnut bread, oatmeal cookies. Get absorbed in measuring out, mixing, folding in, and whisking—flour to your elbows and creative chaos on the countertops. Forget about anything but the kneading and your hands in the dough, hum softly, let the afternoon pass by.

73 · Make a New Friend

Suddenly you realize that you have only known this person for a few hours, but it feels like it has always been. You never know when it will happen, someone just crosses your path and it's there—deep friendship. Other times you long to reach out to that person who seems so humble or refreshingly careless. Say "Hi, I don't know you but..." Would you dare? Some friends you only see at the supermarket checkout, you choose to smile once, and now the cashier lights up when you enter the line. Strike up a conversation with that fellow commuter you see every morning—you may find a kindred spirit.

74 · Celebrate Autumn

I keep an eye on the leaves each year—how far the Japanese maple has come, the birches, the cherry trees. They have the brightest colors once they turn in scarlet red, golden yellow, burnt orange. Jagged edges, long slender tips, and heart shapes. I fill my pockets, hang them like mobiles in the window, leave them in books. The short, vibrant season of turning leaves is swept off the branches with the first blustery rain, so I celebrate autumn outside on a dry, sunny day. Shuffling through drifts, jumping into piles, crumbling a fragrant handful. What do you cherish in autumn?

75 ❧ Let Your Imagination Out

Dark and rainy afternoons are perfect for spending indoors, don't you think? You could spend the day with paintings in an art gallery, explore the exhibitions of a museum, or browse the books at an indoor market. Go to your favorite spot in the library, bring a notebook to the corner café, or watch a long film at the cinema. Explore worlds that are only reached by intrepid travel, sow seeds in your mind that may bloom come spring. What creative places are there to go where your imagination can roam free?

76 ❧ Dance

Some songs just tug at your feet. One chord strikes and dares your heart to a race of escalating drumbeats. Your hands start moving, soon your head begins too. A tap and a twirl and your feet have stopped resisting. Sway those hips, nod to the beat, let it go. You know how to dance, of course you do. The rhythm will tease you, go with it or not. Jump up and down, waltz through your kitchen, move like you've never moved before. Let yourself go, nobody's watching.

77 ॐ *Learn Something New*

Do you pore over course catalogs come September? A photography class, beginner's French. Sitting with your pen ready over a fresh notebook, the afternoon light fading in the classroom, and a term of absorbing lectures ahead of you. Scuba diving, how to tango or fix a car engine. Looking forward to pottery class on Tuesdays, Qigong lessons on Fridays. After a few weeks a difficult move begins to flow or a concept suddenly makes sense and you can't wait to learn more, practice more. What will you learn this year? Woodworking, sign language, how to play the violin?

78 · Go to a Farmer's Market

What are you getting? Glossy pumpkins with those ragged stripes? Silky pale endives, slender haricots verts? Little jars of honey, handwritten labels. Sweet potatoes that go golden and papery in the oven. Dark zucchini with bunches of basil and thyme. Butternut squash, plum-colored onions, clouds of cauliflower. Leeks peeking out of your wicker basket, the last of the summer tomatoes in paper bags. Take your time at each stand—weigh a squash in your hand, pick the reddest apples, choose the curly parsley. Buy the last jar of blackberry jam and add it to your heavy basket.

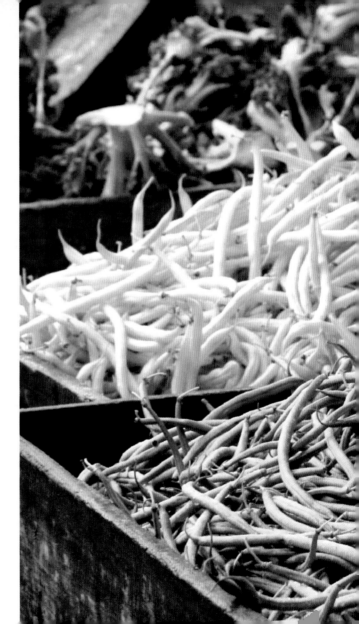

79 ✦ Do in Secret

Stash a loving note in someone's
mitten, do the cleaning unbidden,
or donate an anonymous sum.
Hide words of encouragement for
strangers to find, leave a present on
the doorstep. Sneak flowers onto
someone's work desk, write a love
letter. You'll have to use all your stealth
and sense of adventure and expect
nothing more than a glimpse of the
look on her face or rumors that don't
include you. Outwardly you may
receive nothing but in your chest,
the only one to know, that knowledge
will glow.

80 ✦ Breakfast in Bed

Dark still? Rain on the windowpane?
Why not stay a little longer? Wrap
the duvet closer, have a cup of tea.
Add something small and sweet, the
morning paper, and a slow waking up.
Let the day come to you, watch the
light grow. Ideas of what a lazy Sunday
requires will become clearer, just wait.
There is time to daydream, imagine,
and be open to the unexpected.
What safer place to recharge and
hatch daring plans than in bed?

81 · Bring Autumn Inside

My pockets fill up with chestnuts, acorns, and hazelnuts on autumn walks. Small, shiny shapes that fit nicely in your hand, intricate textures on twigs blown down. Rich reds in berries and rosehips, black in dark elderberries and dusty blue sloe. There is so much to pick up off the ground in autumn, ripe for the taking. Bowls and trays and windowsills fill up with finds. This year I am making a wreath out of it all—fitting twigs and berries and nuts together and keeping it for a while. Nature is ever-changing, soon it will be time to give back what I borrowed.

82 · Try New Recipes

I'd been wanting to bake a quiche for a long time, but never got around
to it, a bit too intimidated. Dishes that require several steps do that to me.
As do unfamiliar ingredients with exotic names, unknown vegetables I pick
up in the fresh produce section. I falter, shifting from one foot to the other,
finally putting the artichoke down again. I love poring over cookbooks, but
turning the stove on and starting takes more. So the challenge is, try more.
Go back for that artichoke, pull out the flour for a quiche crust. What new
recipes would you try?

83 · Light a Fire

The smell of wood burning, smoke carried on brisk winds in the autumn, is
one of my favorite things. A day of falling into a rhythm of raking and gathering leaves into piles and collecting the twigs blown down in the storms.
Lighting a fire that pitches and dances in swift, happy flames. Crackling,
sighing, and pressing its fragrant wall of warmth against your face. Gazing
into the soothing glow, life falls into place—some things burning away like
the summer leaves, some things finding where they always belonged.

84 *Listen*

Rain pattering on the roof, people chatting below in the street, a plane in the distance, the rustle of leaves on the sidewalk. Jazz playing somewhere in an apartment above, dinner sizzling in a pan. Did you ever sit by the window and just listen? Include everything, even things that you would otherwise find distracting. Lean back and let the world carry on while you just experience using your ears. Widen the circle of your perception, letting the distant and subtle sounds join the close by and boisterous. Perhaps they'll create their music together.

85 *Spruce Up*

Summer has gone. Your barefoot feet are thick-skinned and your hair dry after endless saltwater dips in the sun. Time to wipe the sand off your shoulders and step indoors, pour a long, hot bath. Scrub off the remnants of sweaty days, lather up and rinse out. Drop essential oils in the water, prop your feet up, and let lavender or rosemary do their work. Give your hair something nourishing, moisturize your thirsty skin. Pay your cuticles some attention, rub your soles with balm until soft and smooth. Step out glossy-haired and glowing, ready for the cooler weather.

86 Everyday Magic

Everyday magic lies in the little things and sometimes the extraordinary. Some things you remember always—the unexpected, impossible, and marvelous. A moonlight swim, coincidences too amazing to analyze, the moment your daughter was born. Other things just blaze a fleeting spark through a dull Tuesday afternoon, utterly mundane perhaps, but making all the difference. Spotting that rogue red balloon hurtling off into the sky, hearing your favorite song at just the right time. What sparks up your day? Keep your eyes open, let the everyday magic in.

87 ✻ *Let Go*

When the dry, sunny part of autumn is gone and the northerly wind has come swooping down, life changes yet again. The branches go bare, the grass falls asleep under a leaf blanket, nature pares down and simplifies. Energies are pulled in, sap flows closer to the core, animals burrow into warm nests. We pull our coats closer, curl up indoors, and draw our minds inward. It's the season of letting go. What aspects of your life have reached a ripe old age? What needs to be shed to live again in spring? Like the trees, come up with a way to let go of your shriveled leaves—throw scribbled notes in the bonfire, shout your good-byes to the wind, plunk a pebble for each in the stream.

Early Winter

88 · *Hibernate*

We bundle up warm, cup steaming soups in our hands, curl up small under blankets, and go to bed earlier in the cold months. Gathering our reserves and conserving our strength like a bear in hibernation. It's part of the natural cycle of the seasons to slow down and go inward, doing less. A nap in the lull of the afternoon, puttering around in the quiet, stealing a moment to stare out the window at the leisurely fall of snow. Let your body and mind have a rest. Go easy on yourself, you're allowed.

89 · *Winter Celebration*

Winter is here the morning I put on mittens. When the grass crunches with frost and my breath leaves clouds in the air. The morning feels new, a clear, high sky rolled in with crisp weather and a fresh start. Autumn's plain brown is covered in dainty white and decorated with intricate patterns. The chilly air nips my cheeks, rosy and cool. When the afternoon turns dark I'll make some hot chocolate and bring a blanket to the armchair, with an absorbing book. That is my celebration of the cold season—what is yours?

90 ❧ Indoors Garden

One of my favorite books as a child was about a boy who offered to look after all his neighbors' houseplants when they were away on vacation. The house slowly filled up and his parents began complaining. The TV wasn't visible behind the fronds, the bathroom was a steaming jungle, and everywhere, everywhere there was green. What a delightful way to live, I thought, in an indoors garden, and began collecting plants as soon as I grew up. In winter, especially, my window ledges fill up with little trees, vines climbing up to the ceiling, ivy tumbling down.

91 ❧ Poems, Fairy Tales, and Detective Stories

Blustery days call for a juicy story, don't you think? Sink into the cushions and disappear into worlds where the rules for gray days in November don't apply. Fairy tales rich in magic, folklore, and possibility. Detective stories with dodgy characters and brilliant minds. Classic novels with horse-drawn carriages and impeccable manners. Intrigues and love stories, bravery and treachery. Poems that dare you to live a richer life or make you laugh out loud. What books do you disappear into?

92 ❧ Listen to Music

Music follows me around my day. Louis Armstrong gets me grinning in the morning. Rambunctious gypsy music and I do a happy dance over the cooking. Work flows by to the steady heartbeat of backing drums. When the excitement can't be contained any longer, turn up the volume and bounce on the spot. Familiar chords soothe my tired mind at night and sometimes a melody is the only thing that lets me cry. Leave your surroundings behind and follow the flute through a sonata. Lose yourself in an Indian chant or the Beastie Boys.

Light

What do you light in the mornings? When you can't see out the window and the floor is so cold. Before the oatmeal has got started or the coffee brewed. I love the sound of a match striking and the smell, a hint of smoke before I light the burners and the flame swells. Here and there, one after the other, candles flickering to life on the kitchen table. Perhaps you turn on the fairy lights, waking up to sparkle. Maybe you burn some incense to start the day or spread paper lanterns around the room. Winter is the season of spreading light.

94 Fiery Spice

In Sweden, not so many decades ago, spices were a luxury only afforded for the Christmas celebrations. People saved their finest produce and most expensive ingredients for the end of the year. Saffron, cardamom, and ginger. Cocoa, vanilla pods, cloves, and cinnamon. The baking was done with fine-ground white flour, braided into saffron buns or rolled out for gingerbread. Ingredients were measured out carefully from ornate tins and jars. The house filled up with smells from exotic places never seen and flavors connected solely with this time of year. We still associate many of the spices with wintertime, and their fiery vitality makes my everyday life feel rich. A creamy hot chocolate with cinnamon and chili, sweet chai with cardamom pods and real vanilla.

95 Send Unexpected Presents

I can still remember the first time I received something significant in the mail. I was four and my mom had ordered a collection of Mr. Men figurines from the back of a cereal box, starting off a long, long wait. Oh, that sudden tingle of excitement every time the postman slammed the mailbox lid and the disappointment when there was nothing for me. I still get that surge of possibility whenever a parcel arrives, that child's delight at all the colors, shapes, and textures that could hide inside. Wrapping up something small and beautiful for someone in need of a surprise from the postman makes me almost as excited as the person receiving it.

96 · Taste

Do you remember how as a kid a mouthful used to last forever? For vanilla ice cream that was heavenly, but unfortunately this also applied to green beans. They would be swirled around in your mouth, chewed over and over before they were finally gulped down. You may still avoid green beans but for most things the flavor has improved, wouldn't you say? I don't experience food that way anymore though. I don't savor the mouthfuls even when it's heavenly. I wonder what it would be like to let the roasted potatoes or butternut squash soup swirl around and melt in my mouth. Take my time, get to know the flavors.

97 · Play

It's easy to forget what life used to be like. How there weren't enough hours in the day to fill with new games. Laughter came quickly and easily. We'll never be as close to the ground for rough-and-tumble play ever again, but growing up doesn't have to mean losing that sense of wonder and playfulness. The world could use some of that. What mischief do you get into? What did you never let go of since being a child? Marble collections, unconventional ways of eating spaghetti, a love of Calvin and Hobbes? Don't grow up completely, play a little.

98 ❧ *Invite*

Resist the temptation to make the place spotless (I know, neither can I). Invite as many as can fit by your kitchen table, set out plates and glasses in whatever shapes and sizes you have. Prepare one fragrant stew or several small dishes, sing while you stir. Answer the door, talk over the bubbling pots and pans, let the guests help themselves. Whip up a quick dessert and lick the spoon. Get more cushions for the floor, turn the music up. Laugh out loud until the knocks on the wall tell the time. Make hot chocolate and gather enough cups and mugs. Invite people over more often.

99 ❧ *Create Your Own Christmas Tradition*

Every Christmas growing up we'd go for a walk in the snow on Christmas Eve. Star lanterns would be glowing in the windows all December. One certain day was for baking saffron buns, one looking for the perfect tree. Some TV shows were never missed, some carols always sung along to. Now that I've grown up and moved out I cherish those traditions and have begun adding ones of my own. A day of paper and glue for homemade Christmas cards. Adding another advent calendar for the collection. Some traditions are left to be invented—leaving a gift for someone less fortunate, searching out the street decorations that have the most magical light.

100 ⟡ *Reflect*

What new came into your life this year? What did you leave behind? What did you love with all your heart and what did you endure? Bring it all near, speak to it. Cry with the painful, laugh with the ridiculous. Are there experiences that still need comforting or solid cursing? Let it out before you let it go. Do a crazy little dance for all the times you dared, acknowledge the opportunities you let pass (they'll come again). Remember the small moments that for whatever reason stayed with you. Of all that is spread out before you, pick up the meaningful, leave the cumbersome. Have one last look over your shoulder, move on.